CISCO BAY.

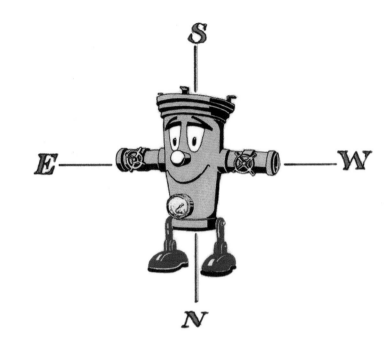

Palace of Fine Arts

Oct. 17, 1989 – major fire
(Beach and Divisadero Sts.)

Marina Green

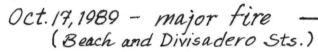

Fort Mason

Frankie
&
The Phoenix

Concept & Model Fabrication by Marc Goldyne
Illustrations by Marc Goldyne & Donald Farnsworth
Story by Nancy Watten Coopersmith

4G Publications
P.O. Box 475382
San Francisco, CA 94147-5382
www.sfphoenix.com

ISBN 978-0-9777588-0-7
ISBN 0-9777588-0-X
Library of Congress Control Number: 2006900676
Printed in China

A portion of the sales of this book will be donated to the SFFD toy program.

The book is dedicated
to the gallant men and women
of the San Francisco Fire Department, (SFFD),
to Frank Blackburn, former Assistant Chief, San Francisco Fire Department,
and to Senator Dianne Feinstein.

Special thanks to Dennis Kennedy,
Marine Engineer, San Francisco Fireboats *Phoenix* and *Guardian*

To Beatrice
This year at FLL is your 1st of
many many to come. we
look forward to seeing you
each year
with love always
Denis & Nancy Kennedy

Introduction

October 17, 1989 was a particularly beautiful day in San Francisco. But shortly after 5 p.m. a huge earthquake struck, and the fate of the entire Marina District would depend on a unique vessel docked at a pier near the Bay Bridge.

The fireboat *Phoenix* is named after a mythological bird that arose from ashes, as did San Francisco after the terrible earthquake and fire back in April 18, 1906. In 1989, when buildings again crumbled and twenty-seven fires broke out, the *Phoenix* took on the biggest and most threatening fire in the Marina District at Divisadero and Beach Streets where flames engulfed a collapsed apartment building and were rapidly spreading. Underground water mains ruptured leaving firefighters without a water supply when they needed it most.

But the *Phoenix* managed to navigate between the sleek and elegant yachts in the narrow marina at the foot of Divisadero Street, and in the glare of emergency lights (all electricity was out), she went into action. At 6,400 gallons a minute, the *Phoenix* pumped water from the Bay through a relay of unique portable hydrants — "Frankies" – that were invented in San Francisco for such an emergency by Frank Blackburn, a now-retired SFFD Assistant Fire Chief. Working together, the *Phoenix* and the portable hydrant system supplied enough water so that, within two hours, the firefighters had a potentially disastrous situation under control.

When I was mayor in the 1980s, there were those who argued that the *Phoenix* was too old and costly and should be retired. Nonsense, I said. With our extended waterfront, she was an essential guardian. (Incidentally, the City added a second fireboat after the '89 quake. Her name: Guardian.)

I am honored to be part of this exceptional book dedicated to San Francisco's firefighters — and "Frankie" and the *Phoenix*. That unforgettable October evening, the *Phoenix* saved the Marina and I salute her… and "Frankie" too.

Dianne Feinstein,
United States Senator

Foreword

The San Francisco Fire Department has played a significant role in the history of our City, and I am proud and honored to serve as its 25th Chief. The San Francisco Fire Department is comprised of 42 Engines, 19 Trucks, and 20 Ambulances, but most importantly, 1700 brave and dedicated men and women. A special component of our Department is the Fireboat *Phoenix*. Our Fireboat stands vigil over our own port and waterfront area, and acts as a guardian for the entire Bay Area. I have been fortunate to have worked in a variety of assignments during my career with the San Francisco Fire Department. Without a doubt, my time working as a Lieutenant, the Commanding Officer, on the Fireboat *Phoenix* has been most memorable and helped me to gain a better understanding and true appreciation of its value to the City it serves.

Few of the many people who visit the City and County of San Francisco and are impressed by its beauty can imagine the way it looked on the evening of October 17, 1989. That evening, a great earthquake shook, resulting in multiple fire, structural, and medical emergencies, jeopardizing hundreds of lives. On that evening, and for days afterwards, the men and women of the San Francisco Fire Department joined forces with our citizens to prevent Mother Nature from taking the City from us. Nowhere was this struggle more evident than the Marina District, located at the foot of the Bay. It was here that the powerful Fireboat *Phoenix* and its valiant crew pumped water from the Bay, through our portable hydrant system, and to the scene of the largest fire in the City, enabling us to prevent the fire from spreading and engulfing the entire Marina District.

Frankie & The Phoenix tells us the story of that night in October when citizens and Firefighters stood shoulder to shoulder to save our City. The story of *Frankie & the Phoenix* is a wonderful way for children and adults to learn more about the San Francisco Fire Department, what we do, and to inspire those in future generations to pursue a career in the Fire Service, a challenging, and rewarding and honorable profession.

In addition to being the Fire Chief, I am also the mother of three young sons, Riley (11) Logan (7) and Sean (5). I can attest to the entertaining and educational way this book introduces the Fire Service, and I hope that you and your children enjoy it as much as we have.

Joanne Hayes-White
Fire Chief
San Francisco Fire Department

*P*hoenix the Fireboat floated quietly in the calm waters by the pier behind Engine Station 35. Her red nozzles drooped, and her usually bright pilot house was quiet and dark.

Large tears ran slowly down her face and fell to the gently rocking deck below.

Frankie, the portable water hydrant, sat on the corner of the pier and tried to cheer up his old friend. "Poor *Phoenix*," he said. "Please don't cry."

"Poor *Phoenix*! Poor *Phoenix*!" screamed the gulls circling overhead in the clear warm October sky. "Poor *Phoenix*! Poor *Phoenix*!" echoed the gulls perched on the station house roof.

All along the waterfront, the word had spread from City Hall to freighter to tanker to tugboat to motor launch to sailboat: "The *Phoenix* is too expensive . . . too old fashioned . . . a waste of money!"

"The City doesn't need me," thought *Phoenix*. She sighed deeply – a deck-rattling, chain-clanking, twin-propeller-churning sigh.

Phoenix thought about the past – those exciting times when her days had been full of fun and adventure.

She remembered all of the fires she had put out along the waterfront, her powerful nozzles shooting water into the roaring flames. She had felt so proud escorting large Navy ships under the Golden Gate Bridge to the cheers of the sailors standing on the decks. She had loved leading parades of sailboats with her plumes of water spraying higher than the tops of the billowing sails.

"It has been an exciting job," thought *Phoenix*, "but now it seems to be coming to an end."

Frankie had his own worries. "Who needs a portable water hydrant?" he thought. "The City already has enough high-pressure hydrants on the streets. With the underground water mains, they can get enough water to fight any fire."

And so, as hands on the Ferry Building clock pointed to a little after five, Frankie and the *Phoenix* prepared to spend another long, quiet evening behind Station House 35.

Suddenly the pier jerked, scraping the *Phoenix'* hull. "Ouch!" cried *Phoenix*, "What was that?"

Frankie stood up. His legs wobbled like Jell-O and his body shook.

There was another hard shake. The pier moved up and down, then sideways. The water churned and splashed. The gulls resting on the roof of the station house took off in a hasty flutter.

Frankie almost fell off the pier. "What's going on?" he cried. He heard the sound of breaking glass and the distant shouts of people crying for help.

Phoenix heard honking horns and screeching brakes as cars, trucks, and buses came to a sudden stop on the elevated freeway that ran along the waterfront. And all the while, the pier lurched and creaked, and the water churned and splashed.

Then . . . all the shaking and honking and screeching and lurching and creaking stopped, and it became very quiet.

The siren from Engine 35 broke the silence as the fire engine roared off to answer an alarm.

Frankie climbed aboard the *Phoenix*. "What's going on?" he asked. "I don't know," said *Phoenix*. "But whatever it is, I don't like it." They waited anxiously by the pier.

Almost an hour later Fireboat Pilot Arvid, Engineer Nate, and Officer Bob hurried out of the fire house and leaped aboard the fireboat.

"What's going on?" demanded the *Phoenix*. "Earthquake!" answered Pilot Arvid as he entered the pilot house. "Biggest quake since 1906," added Engineer Nate, as he prepared to go below and start the *Phoenix*' two engines.

"The City is a mess!" said Officer Bob, releasing the ropes securing the *Phoenix* to the pier. "Buildings have collapsed, and neighborhoods have no water or electricity. And we just got a call from the Marina District; a gas leak has started a big fire that could go out of control!"

With both engines churning, the *Phoenix* pulled away from the dock. Gathering speed, the *Phoenix* entered the open water. Racing along the waterfront, she scanned the shore with anxious eyes.

The great clock on the Ferry Building had stopped, its hands frozen at four minutes past five o'clock. The flagpole at the top of the tower tilted sideways, as if a giant hand had given it a smack. "Look!" shouted Frankie. "The Ferry Building is still shaking!"

"Hurry, *Phoenix*, hurry!" called a group of pelicans flying by. "Follow us! We'll show you the way!"

At full throttle, Frankie and the *Phoenix* sped through the water. The *Phoenix* glanced up. Coit Tower looked very frightened. The biggest skyscrapers along the San Francisco skyline looked frightened, too.

"Hurry up! Hurry up!" they seemed to be saying as clouds of black smoke began to drift across the sky.

"Hurry up! Hurry up!" squawked the Cherry-headed Conures flying down from Telegraph Hill. "Hurry! Hurry!"

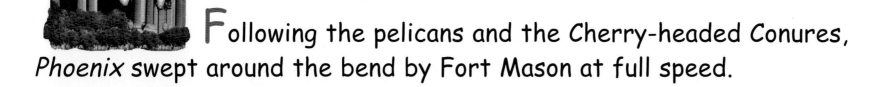Following the pelicans and the Cherry-headed Conures, *Phoenix* swept around the bend by Fort Mason at full speed.

"Wow!" cried Frankie when he saw flames shooting high into the sky.

"Wow!" echoed *Phoenix*, as she headed for the harbor inlet. "Look at that! The Palace of Fine Arts is looking so scared! The whole neighborhood could burn to the ground! This is really serious!"

"Good luck, *Phoenix*! Good luck, Frankie!" cried the pelicans. "Good luck! Good luck!" squawked the Cherry-headed Conures.

Pilot Arvid carefully guided the *Phoenix* around the pleasure boats moored in the harbor. Approaching the floating dock near the seawall, Frankie and the *Phoenix* stared at the flames that were shooting higher and higher, lighting up the evening sky.

"Thank heavens you're here!" called a familiar voice. In the beam of the fireboat searchlight, Frankie and the *Phoenix* spotted Fireman Ted from Engine 35 waving from a floating pier. Along the seawall anxious neighbors waved and waited for help.

"Why aren't you fighting the fire?" shouted *Phoenix* to Fireman Ted.

"Engine crews are working hard, but a burning building collapsed on the high pressure hydrants, and the underground mains are broken!" responded Fireman Ted. "There is no water! There is no water to put out the fire! The engines need a water supply. Frankie, you and the *Phoenix* are our only hope! We have no time to lose!"

Frankie jumped quickly onto the pier where Fireman Ted was standing and ran to the seawall. "I'm ready!" he shouted.

With the help of firefighters and other volunteers, Fireman Ted and Officer Bob connected three-inch diameter hoses – the widest that the *Phoenix* could handle – to a "Y" joint on one of Frankie's arms. They connected a special five-inch diameter hose to Frankie's other arm. "This large hose will supply water to the pumper trucks and other portable hydrants just like you that are nearer the fire," said Fireman Ted.

When all of the hoses were firmly attached, Frankie called out, "OK, *Phoenix*, pump!"

"Pump!" cried Officer Bob, Engineer Nate, and Pilot Arvid.

"Pump!" shouted Fireman Ted and all of the volunteers.

Frankie felt the surge of high pressure water flow through his arms as the *Phoenix'* pumps leaped into action. Pumper trucks linked together more hoses and more portable hydrants that had been brought to them by other fire trucks.

"Finally!" shouted the firemen as powerful streams of water shot from their hoses into the raging fire.

Phoenix pumped and Frankie relayed the water all night long as the firemen doused the towering flames and soaked down hot spots.

"I think it's under control," said Fireman Ted. "Yes!" cried the other fire-fighters and the volunteers as the flames slowly died and the plumes of thick black smoke turned to clouds of white steam.

Slowly the air cleared and, at last, the rising moon became the brightest light in the sky.

It was the next morning when Engineer Nate finally turned off the *Phoenix'* pumps and the firefighters disconnected the hoses.

"We did it!" exclaimed one of the weary firemen.

"Yes, we did it! And you are a hero, Frankie," said a tired firefighter, giving the portable hydrant a grateful pat on the head.

Behind Frankie, volunteers, neighbors, and other firefighters gathered at the seawall.

"Hurray for *Phoenix*!" they cheered. "You saved the Marina! Thank you! Thank you!"

As Frankie and the *Phoenix* headed back to Station House 35, the sun was climbing high in the sky along the waterfront. They smiled happily, because the word was spreading from sailboat to motor launch to tugboat to tanker to freighter to City Hall: "Frankie and the *Phoenix* saved the Marina!"

"Heroes!" called the pelicans flying overhead. "Heroes!" answered the gull perched on the *Phoenix*' tower monitor. The gull sitting on the *Phoenix*' prow smiled with pride.

"*Phoenix*, you did it!" said Frankie.

"No, Frankie, WE did it!" answered *Phoenix*. "I think WE may be needed after all!"

And *Phoenix* laughed joyfully; a deck-rattling, chain-clanking, twin-propeller-churning laugh.

S.F.F.D. PORTABLE HYDRANT

Portable hydrant ("Frankie") developed in 1985
by Asst. Chief Frank Blackburn (ret.) SFFD.

Acknowledgements

This children's book is the product of a collective dream, and I want to acknowledge family and friends who turned the dream into reality.

My wonderful energetic and supportive wife, Gail, persisted in encouraging me to create a children's picture book about the portable hydrant system and the fireboat that saved our Marina District from complete devastation following the 1989 Loma Prieta Earthquake.

Don Farnsworth, a master printmaker, artist, papermaker, and wizard of computer graphics took the caricature models I created of Frankie and the fireboat Phoenix along with multiple scenic photographs and transformed them into computer-generated pigment ink-jet prints on rag paper that I then overlaid with watercolor to create the final images for this book.

Nancy Coopersmith, a talented writer and bookmaker composed the story based both on the illustrations as well as her own research on San Francisco's portable hydrant system and the fireboat. Her efforts completed the transition from dream to reality.

Dennis Kennedy, Marine Engineer for the Phoenix, provided invaluable advice, information, support, and enthusiasm. He arranged several excursions on the fireboat so we could photograph the unique San Francisco shoreline through the eyes of "Frankie and the Phoenix". These images became the resource for the book plates.

I thank all of you for your unique contributions that made this undertaking such a wonderful adventure.

Marc Goldyne
San Francisco
October 17, 2004

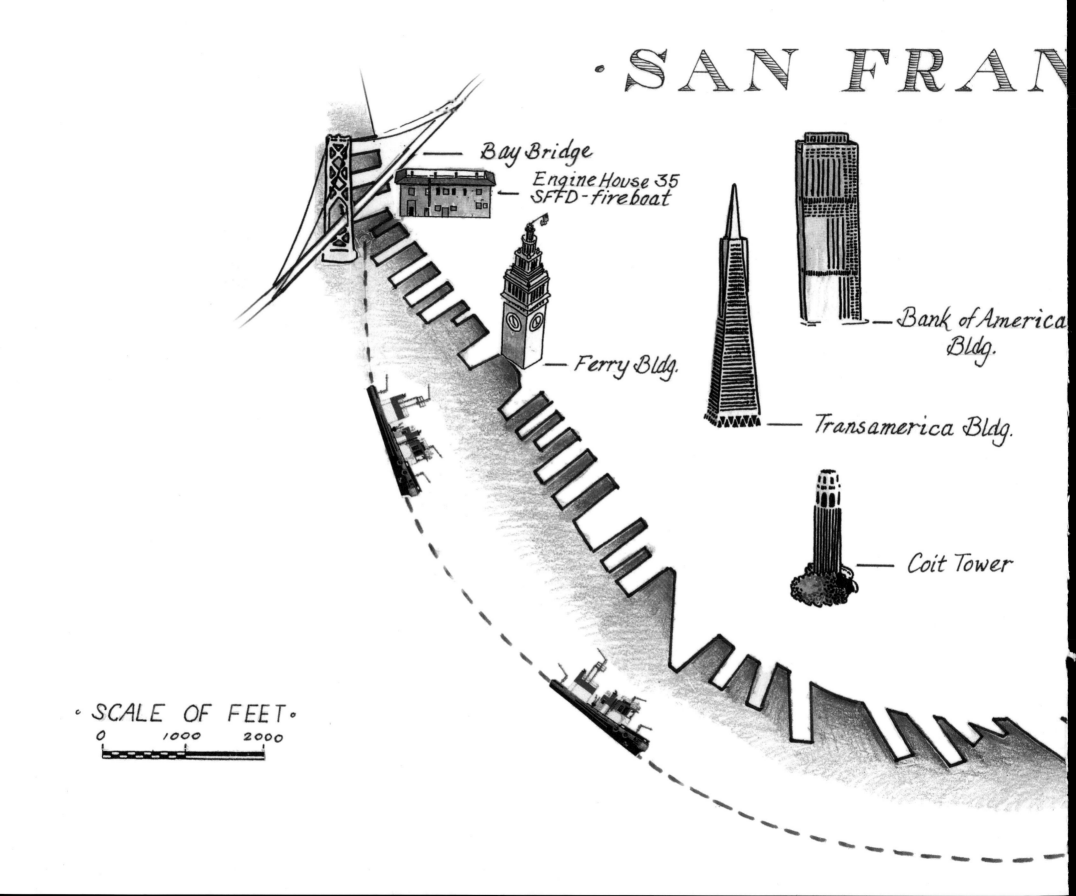

·SAN FRAN

Bay Bridge

Engine House 35
SFFD - fireboat

Ferry Bldg.

Transamerica Bldg.

Bank of America
Bldg.

Coit Tower

·SCALE OF FEET·

0   1000   2000